MARTIN LUTHER

A Monk Changes the World

Artwork
Johannes Saurer

Text and colour
Ulrike Albers

EISLEBEN 1483

Martin Luther goes to the local primary school in Mansfeld. His upbringing and education are extremely strict and religious. At school the teachers are allowed to beat the children. Martin suffers terribly as a result of this strict upbringing.

Mansfeld 1490

Schooldays

ERFURT 1500
Martin works hard and, in 1501, is admitted to the university to study law. His father wants him to become a lawyer.
However, something happens which is to change his life for ever.
On 2nd July, 1505, while returning to Erfurt from his parents' house, he encounters a ferocious thunderstorm.
Saint Anna, please save me and I swear I will become a monk!
Martin reveals his plans for the future to his father.
You can't do that! I have put all my hopes in you and have worked so hard so that you can study law.
My decision is final! It's my vocation and I can't change it!

Fasting, prayer and work

WITTENBERG 1508

Life carries on. In 1508, Luther is transferred to Wittenberg by his order. There he studies theology until 1512, gains his doctorate and teaches at the University of Wittenberg as a professor.

By saying that you call into question everything that we do, every aspect of monastic life.
I have found the answer to all my questions. That is brilliant!
No, I don't think so!
I would like to exchange ideas with the great thinkers of our age. With Johann von Staupitz, Wenzeslaus Linck, Nikolaus von Amsdorf and Karlstadt.
The scholars agree : the Church is going about things the wrong way !
It can't carry on like this.
It is easy to exploit people's fears of going to hell after death.
Ecclesiastical offices can be bought. That's how Albrecht von Brandenburg has come to be both Archbishop of Magdeburg and Mainz at the same time. That's simply not allowed!
The peasants are living in utter poverty and destitution.
The bishops spend money like water and live in the lap of luxury.
In 1514, Luther is appointed preacher at the town church of St. Mary's in Wittenberg.
If God expected righteousness of us, we would all be lost!
God grants us grace!

The Tyranny of the Church

In 1517, Luther writes his theses in Latin.
That's ended up longer than I thought. 95 arguments against the arbitrariness of the Church.
I'm really looking forward to all the discussions.
It was common practice for scholars in Wittenberg to fix notices to the door of the castle church.
I hope I will be able to bring about some change with my 95 theses.
Friends of Luther are so impressed with his 95 theses that they translate them into German, print and distribute them without Luther's knowledge.
Johannes Gutenberg made this possible with his new printing method.
That is extraordinary indeed!
Forgiveness is only possible through the grace of God.
No charitable works or good deeds will guarantee you a place in Heaven.

Augsburg 1518

Luther's ideas find more and more followers. He is the leader of a movement which wants to reform the Church. But the pope expels him from the Church and, on 3rd January, 1521, he is excommunicated by papal bull. Nevertheless, more and more people join the movement of the Reformation. Among them is Justus Jonas, a friend of Luther's and dean of the castle church in Wittenberg.

WORMS 1521

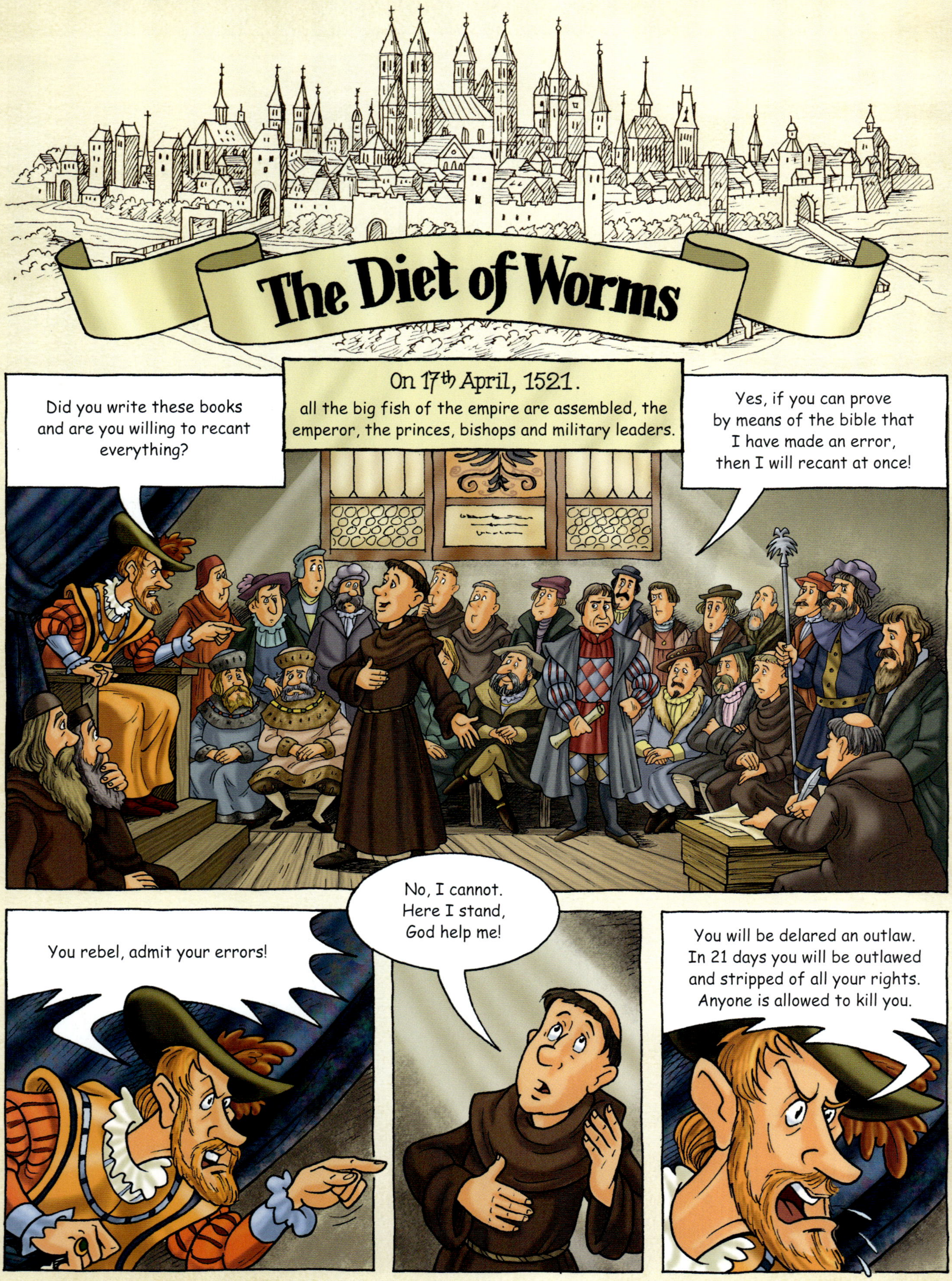

The Diet of Worms
On 17th April, 1521.
all the big fish of the empire are assembled, the emperor, the princes, bishops and military leaders.
Did you write these books and are you willing to recant everything?
Yes, if you can prove by means of the bible that I have made an error, then I will recant at once!
You rebel, admit your errors!
No, I cannot. Here I stand, God help me!
You will be delared an outlaw. In 21 days you will be outlawed and stripped of all your rights. Anyone is allowed to kill you.

I am finished!
Martin!
Spalatin, my friend, what are you doing here?
I am here in my capacity as privy secretary to Frederick the Wise and I am to tell you that he is on your side and will protect you.
Give my thanks to our elector.
On the return journey ...
Stop!
Luther or your life!
That's Martin Luther there! Take him, but spare us!

Luther is seized and carried away.
How could you betray him?
They were the pope's henchmen, I'm sure. They would have killed us all otherwise.
Don't worry! I'm taking you to safety.
Elector Frederick the Wise had planned the abduction in order to protect Martin Luther.
I don't like this at all! I want to return to Wittenberg!
Your comrades have everything under control. Philipp Melanchthon is leading them and Johannes Bugenhagen is organizing everything. You are going to hide in Wartburg Castle.
But ...

You should be pleased that our elector is taking you out of the limelight for a while. You are an outlaw without rights. Anyone could kill you with impunity.
WARTBURG CASTLE 1521
Hello, my dear Luther. It's splendid that you are here! Let your hair and beard grow so that no one will recognize you! We will call you Junker Jörg in order to conceal your true identity.
But I can't just sit around here!
Then make use of the time to do something that you always wanted to do. I will make sure that you are well looked after.
I am starting to translate the New Testament from Greek into German.
That's a good idea! How are your gout and your constipation?
This constant pain! I can't see it ever getting better.

Luther works for weeks as if possessed. He is totally exhausted and overworked.
One night the Devil appears to him again.
You poor, pathetic little man! You will never achieve anything in this world!
Get lost, you monster!

On 20th September, 1522, the first printed copies of the New Testament are given to Elector Frederick the Wise. The pope bans the reading of the book.

Back in Wittenberg ...
Restrain yourselves! Remain peaceful!
We are not going to let the Church continue robbing us.
In everything that we do we have God's word on our side. We mustn't allow ourselves to be put in the wrong!
Later Luther meets with Melanchthon.
If we are all equal before God, then everyone can play his part in the successful running of the community.
Yes, but a bit of education wouldn't do any harm.

Children are the future of the community. Singing together of God and life forms a bond between people and makes them strong. Children have to sing! Even before they can read! A good song stirs every heart.
If every boy and every girl were able to read the bible themselves, they wouldn't have to rely on the authorities when it comes to the question of establishing the truth.
You are absolutely right! We really need schools for the people.
I like that idea. Let me work on that plan.
They think about how they can improve every area of life. The reform of social welfare is achieved by the introduction of a "communal fund".
We should have communal funds that we can use to pay for charitable work and education. We can use some of the fortune of the old Church for that.
And we can collect new money if we ask the congregation at every service to donate some money for the poor.

Luther and the Peasants' War

Luther turns his back on the peasants and their cause. He even advocates the merciless persecution of the rebels by the counts.
The drawstring shoe, or Bundschuh, is depicted on the peasants' flag as a symbol that the peasants are in revolt and together are advancing against their rulers. On 15th May, 1525, at the decisive battle near Frankenhausen, more than 5,000 peasants are slaughtered by their princes and rulers.
Luther feels in part to blame, something which haunts him for the rest of his life.

Luther's Marriage to Katharina von Bora

What do you want me to do?
You don't have to do anything. I will get some hens and geese and I will turn the garden into a vegetable garden. Then you can invite your comrades to visit.
Luther goes to get money from his housekeeping purse.
Stop!
Not like that! I need to know how much money I have to spend on housekeeping.
You're right, of course. I'm so grateful that you manage everything so efficiently.
Luther and Katharina live in a household with their six children, one of Katharina's relatives and with Luther's sister's six children. Sometimes Luther's students board with them, which helps them to make ends meet. The Luthers' house is always full of life.

SCHMALKALDEN 1531

The Schmalkaldic League

Many former followers such as Johann Agricola, Erasmus of Rotterdam and Zwingli, turn against Luther, accusing him of making compromises with the princes.
When things get serious, you chicken out!
There's no point talking to you!
We Baptists are doing it right!
All nonsense! I'm going to found my own church in Switzerland!
Luther is tired, disappointed and plagued by terrible pain. He has done a great deal of good in his life, but he got a lot of things wrong as well. For example, the reformer called for the death of Turks, peasants, prostitutes, those of a different faith and Jews.
Well, you pathetic little man, you brought unhappiness on many people!
I am at the end of my tether. Everything hurts and there is so much left to do!
HAHAHA!
Remember the peasants, that you let down, all of them dead!
I'm keeping a place free for you with me in Purgatory!

HARTENFELS CASTLE 1544

TORGAU

Torgau was the favourite residence of the elector's court. It is here that the Reformation was given protection and, later, was granted military support by Elector John Frederick, the Magnanimous.

The Dispute of the Mansfeld Counts

Luther is in demand everywhere. On 17th January, 1546, Luther sets out for Eisleben, the town where he was born. There he settles an inheritance dispute between his friend and supporter of the reform movement, Count Albrecht, and his Catholic brother.

Luther's Death

Luther dies in the early hours of the morning of 18th February.

His funeral procession travels via Halle to Wittenberg, where he is interred in the castle church of All Saints.

His friends Melanchthon and Bugenhagen deliver a commemorative speech in Wittenberg four days later.

The World in about 1500

The Transition from the Middle Ages to the Modern Age

1450: Johannes Gutenberg invents a printing process which enables books to be printed rapidly and at a low cost.

1492: The first globe is constructed

1500: Peter Henlein invents the pocket watch.

About 1514: Copernicus discovers that the earth revolves around the sun.

The Life of Luther

1483	Born in Eisleben
from 1490	School in Mansfeld, Magdeburg and Eisenach
1501-1505	Studied law in Erfurt
1505	Monk in Erfurt
1507	Ordination to the priesthood
1508-1512	Studied theology in Wittenberg. Awarded doctorate.
1517	Theses nailed to door of church
1521	Outlawed and in hiding at Wartburg Castle
1522	Return to Wittenberg
1525	Marriage to Katharina von Bora
1534	Publication of German translation of bible
1546	Died in Eisleben

Leonardo da Vinci develops pumps and flying machines among other things.

1492: Christopher Columbus lands in America.

1519-1521: Fernao de Magalhaes becomes the first person to sail around the world.